SUPERMAN ORIGAMI™

AMAZING FOLDING PROJECTS FEATURING THE MAN OF STEEL

Published by Capstone Press in 2015
A Capstone Imprint
1710 Roe Crest Drive
North Mankato, Minnesota 56003
www.capstonepub.com

STAR35425

Library of Congress Cataloging-in-Publication Data
Montroll, John, author.
  Superman origami : amazing folding projects featuring the man
of steel / by John Montroll ; Superman created by Jerry Siegel
and Joe Shuster.
       pages cm.—(DC super heroes. DC origami)
  Summary: "Provides instructions and diagrams for folding
origami models of characters, objects, and symbols related to
Superman"—Provided by publisher.
  Audience: Age 8–12.
  Audience: Grades 4–6.
  Includes bibliographical references.
  ISBN 978-1-4914-1787-4 (library binding)
  ISBN 978-1-4914-7594-2 (eBook PDF)
1. Origami—Juvenile literature. 2. Superman (Fictitious
character)—Juvenile literature. 3. Superheroes in art—Juvenile
literature. 4. Handicraft—Juvenile literature. I. Siegel, Jerry,
1914–1996, creator. II. Shuster, Joe, creator. III. Title.
  TT872.5.M68 2015
  736.982—dc23   2015003762

Editorial Credits

Editor and Model Folder: Christopher Harbo
Designer: Lori Bye
Art Directors: Bob Lentz and Nathan Gassman
Contributing Writers: Donald Lemke and Michael Dahl
Folding Paper Illustrator: Min Sung Ku
Production Specialist: Kathy McColley

Photo Credits

Capstone Studio/Karon Dubke, all photos

Printed in the United States of America in North Mankato, MN.
052015 008823CGF15

TABLE OF CONTENTS

The Power of Paper Folding 4
Symbols 6   Basic Folds 7

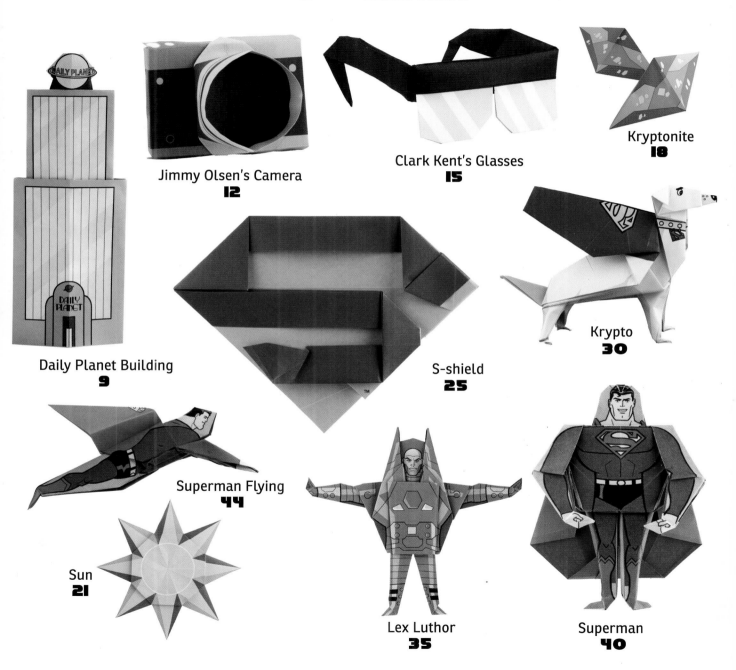

The Power of Paper Folding

When it comes to superpowers, the Man of Steel has no equal. He can stop a runaway train with his strength, see through brick walls with his X-ray vision, and fly anywhere in the world in a matter of seconds. But if Superman squared off against a single piece of paper, could he fold it into a shard of Kryptonite or an S-shield symbol? If not, then you have an ability even Superman can't match. You have the power of paper folding!

Through the art of origami, you can now transform paper into the most remarkable collection of objects, symbols, and figures ever created for the World's Greatest Super Hero. From Clark Kent's glasses and Jimmy Olsen's camera to Lex Luthor and Superman himself, every model you fold will amaze your friends. After all, who could resist a paper version of Krypto the Super-Dog or Superman in flight?

Whether you're a first-time folder or you have years of origami experience, this collection will help you succeed. The folding diagrams are drawn in the internationally approved Randlett-Yoshizawa style. This style is easy to follow once you learn the basic folds outlined in the pages to come. The models are also ranked and organized for their level of difficulty: one star for simple, two stars for intermediate, and three stars for complex. By working through the collection from simplest to most complex, you'll build your folding skills. With patience and practice, you can become an origami super hero!

So choose a favorite project, grab a square of paper, and behold the power of origami!

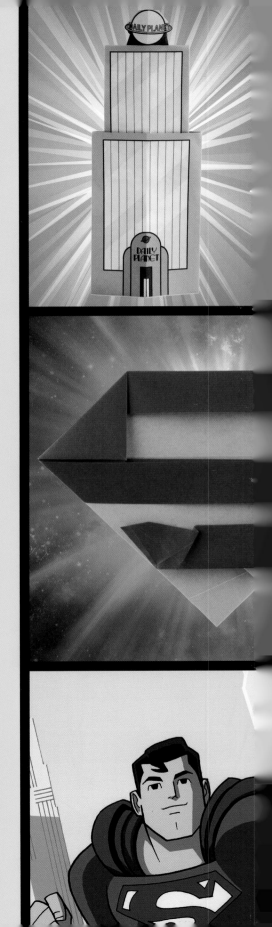

Symbols

Lines

— — — — — — — —   Valley fold, fold in front.

—··—··—··—··—··—   Mountain fold, fold behind.

————————   Crease line.

·····················   X-ray or guide line.

Arrows

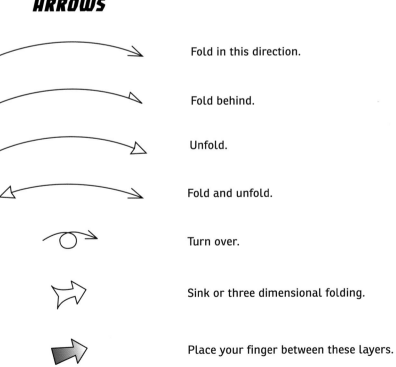

Fold in this direction.

Fold behind.

Unfold.

Fold and unfold.

Turn over.

Sink or three dimensional folding.

Place your finger between these layers.

Basic Folds

Pleat Fold

Fold back and forth. Each pleat is composed of one valley and mountain fold. Here are two examples.

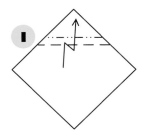

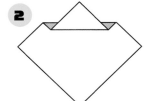

Pleat-fold.

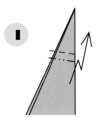

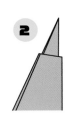

Pleat-fold.

Squash Fold

In a squash fold, some paper is opened and then made flat. The shaded arrow shows where to place your finger.

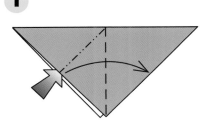

Squash-fold.

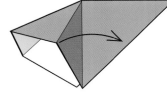

A 3D step.

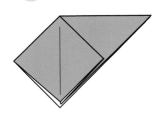

Inside Reverse Fold

In an inside reverse fold, some paper is folded between layers. The inside reverse fold is generally referred to as a reverse fold. Here are two examples.

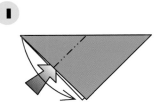

Reverse-fold.

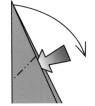

Reverse-fold.

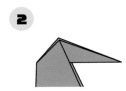

Petal Fold

In a petal fold, one point is folded up while two opposite sides meet each other.

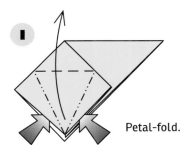

Petal-fold.

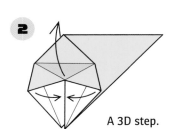

A 3D step.

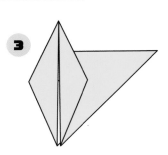

CRIMP FOLD

A crimp fold is a combination of two reverse folds. Open the model slightly to form the crimp evenly on each side. Here are two examples.

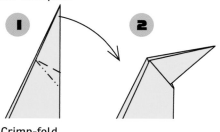

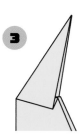

Crimp-fold.

Crimp-fold.

A 3D step.

SPREAD SQUASH FOLD

A cross between a squash fold and sink fold, some paper in the center is spread apart and then made flat.

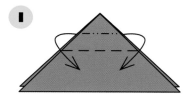

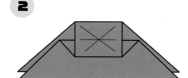

Spread-squash-fold.

PRELIMINARY FOLD

The preliminary fold is the starting point for many models. The maneuver in step 3 occurs in many other models.

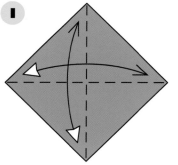

Fold and unfold.
Turn over.

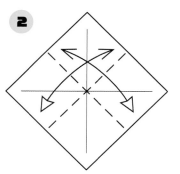

Fold and unfold.

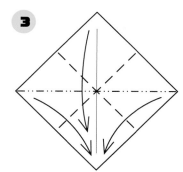

Collapse the square by bringing the four corners together.

This is 3D.

Preliminary Fold

DAILY PLANET BUILDING

An icon of the Metropolis skyline, the Daily Planet Building is home to the city's most reputable newspaper, the *Daily Planet*. Beneath the building's distinctive globe, the World's Greatest Hero, Superman, hides in plain sight as mild-mannered reporter Clark Kent. Alongside fellow reporter Lois Lane, Clark gets the scoop on the day's top stories—when he's not too busy saving the day, of course!

LEVEL: ★☆☆

1

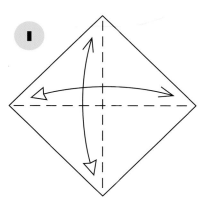

Fold and unfold.

2

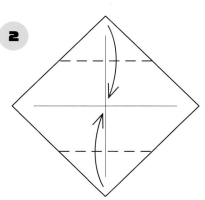

Fold to the center.

3

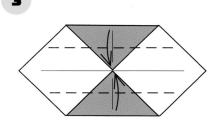

Fold to the center.

4

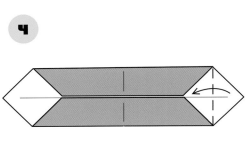

Fold to the left.
Rotate model 90°.

5

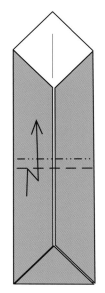

Pleat-fold.
Valley-fold along
the crease.

6

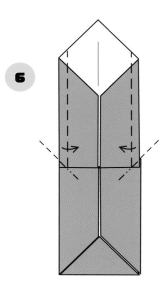

Make thin
squash folds.

7

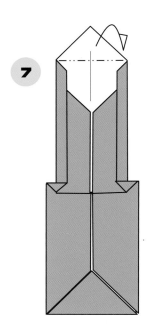

Fold behind.

8

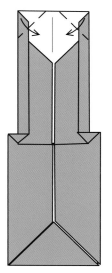

Fold toward
the center.

9

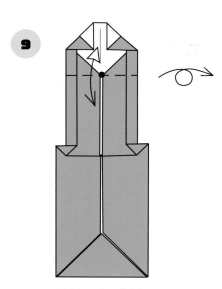

Fold and unfold.
Turn over.

10

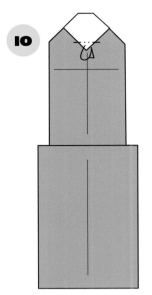

Fold behind.

11

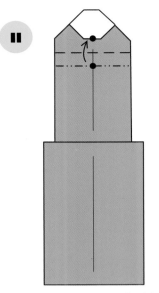

Pleat-fold. Mountain-fold
along the crease.

12

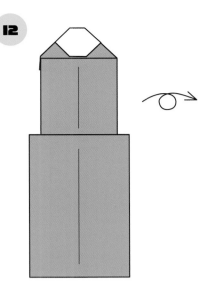

Turn over.

13

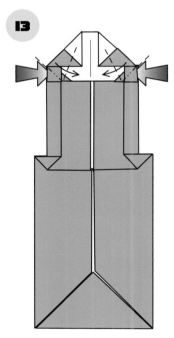

Make squash
folds under the
white layers.

14

Bend slightly so the
building is 3D and
can stand. Turn over.

15

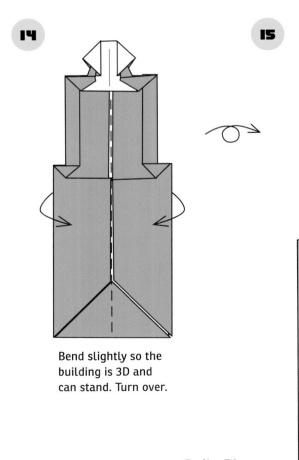

Daily Planet
Building

JIMMY OLSEN'S CAMERA

Jimmy Olsen, cub reporter for the *Daily Planet*, has no idea that his coworker Clark Kent is also his hero, Superman. Nonetheless, the red-caped champion and his redheaded buddy make a terrific team. Whether the Man of Steel battles Lex Luthor's latest evil invention or rescues the victims of a natural disaster, Jimmy is on the scene. With his trusty camera, he snaps perfect pics for fast-breaking scoops. And when the inquisitive kid's photos land him in hot water with crime lords or alien invaders, never fear! Jimmy signals his super-friend with his special wristwatch. Faster than a camera flash, Superman swoops in to protect his pal.

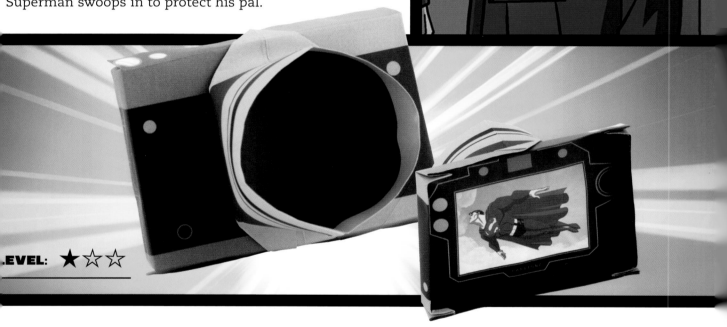

LEVEL: ★☆☆

1

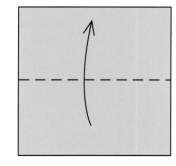

Fold in half.

2

Fold a thin strip.
Repeat behind.

3

Unfold.

4

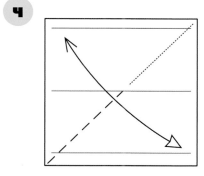

Fold and unfold
on the bottom.

5

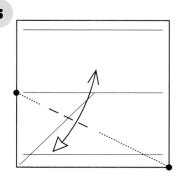

Fold and unfold
by the diagonal.

6

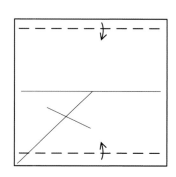

Fold along the creases.

7

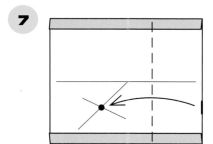

Fold to the dot.

8

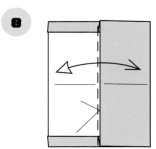

Fold and unfold.

9

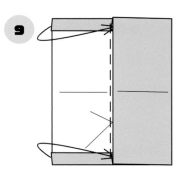

Tuck inside.

10

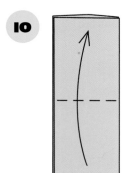

Fold along the crease
and rotate model.

11

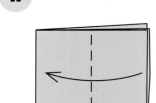

Fold the top flap.

12

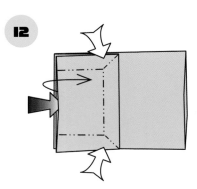

Open the flap on the
left, bring it to the center,
and make the rim round.
The model will be 3D.

13

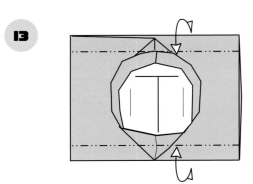

Fold and unfold all
the layers together.

14

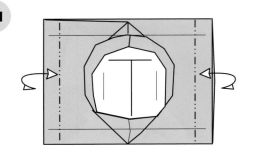

Fold and unfold all
the layers together.

15

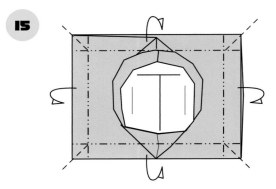

Fold the edges to
make the camera 3D.

16

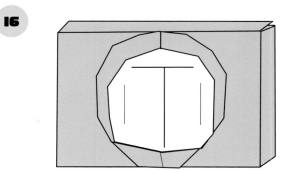

Jimmy Olsen's Camera

CLARK KENT'S GLASSES

Superman's alter ego as mild-mannered reporter for the *Daily Planet*, Clark Kent, allows him to keep an ear and eye on breaking news. From natural disasters to criminal activity, the Man of Steel stays tuned in to major emergencies around the globe. Part of his disguise is a simple pair of glasses. People who see a guy with specs would never guess that he has X-ray or heat vision. Or that a quiet man like Kent could transform into the World's Greatest Hero in the blink of an eye!

LEVEL: ★★☆

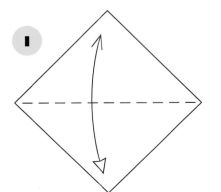

Fold and unfold.

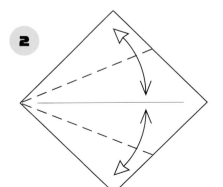

Fold and unfold.

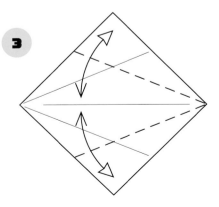

Fold and unfold.

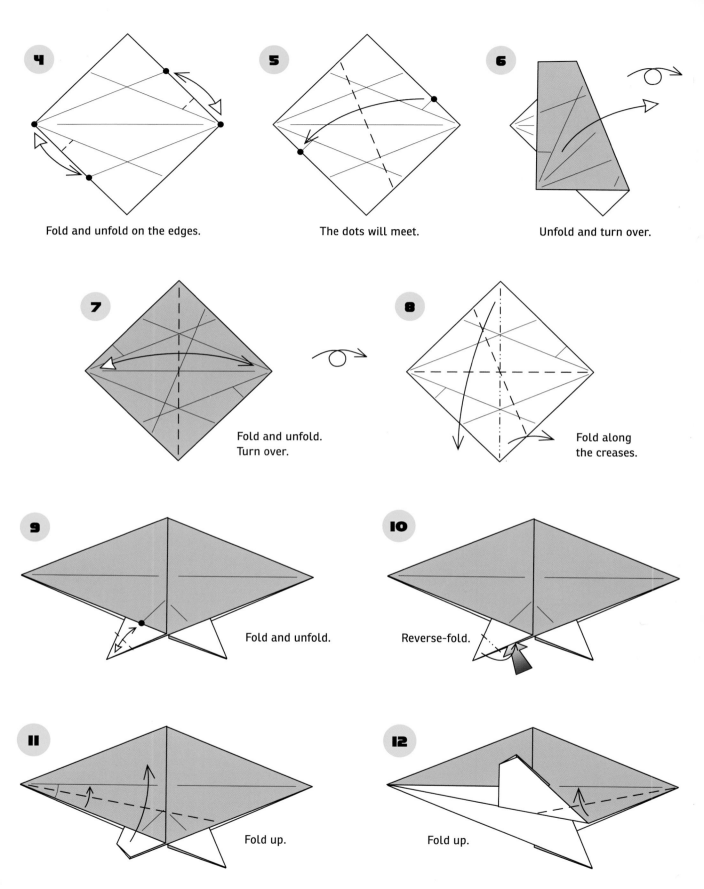

4 Fold and unfold on the edges.

5 The dots will meet.

6 Unfold and turn over.

7 Fold and unfold. Turn over.

8 Fold along the creases.

9 Fold and unfold.

10 Reverse-fold.

11 Fold up.

12 Fold up.

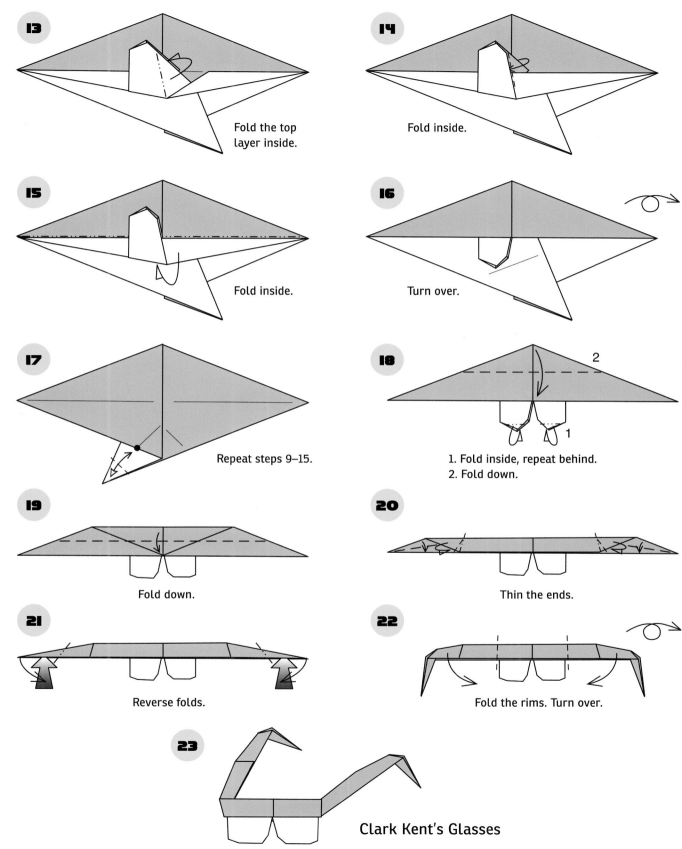

13 Fold the top layer inside.

14 Fold inside.

15 Fold inside.

16 Turn over.

17 Repeat steps 9–15.

18
1. Fold inside, repeat behind.
2. Fold down.

19 Fold down.

20 Thin the ends.

21 Reverse folds.

22 Fold the rims. Turn over.

23

Clark Kent's Glasses

KRYPTONITE

The Man of Steel has many superpowers: flight, freeze breath, heat vision, X-ray vision, and super-strength. He also has one terrible weakness—Kryptonite! When Superman's home planet exploded, fragments of Krypton scattered throughout the universe. Some shards even landed on Earth in the form of meteorites. These glowing, radioactive rocks come in a variety of colors, each having a unique effect on the Man of Steel. The most common form, Green Kryptonite, drains many of his superpowers, leaving him dangerously vulnerable to his vilest enemies.

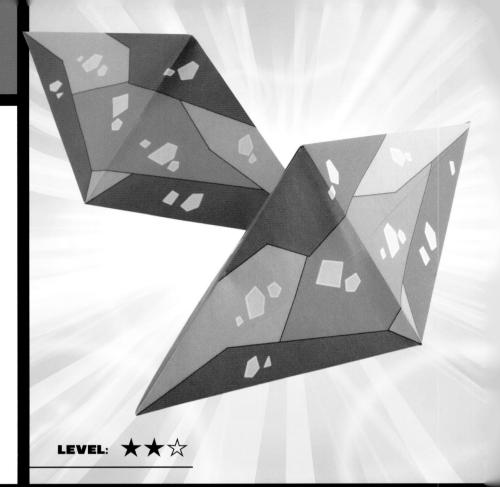

LEVEL: ★ ★ ☆

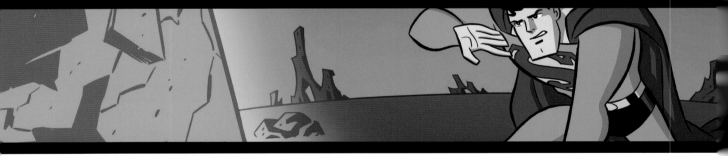

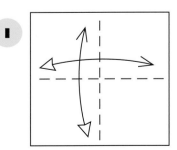

1 Fold and unfold.

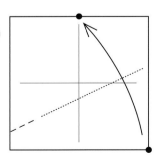

2 Bring the lower corner to the dot. Crease on the left.

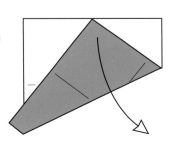

3 Unfold and rotate model 180°.

18

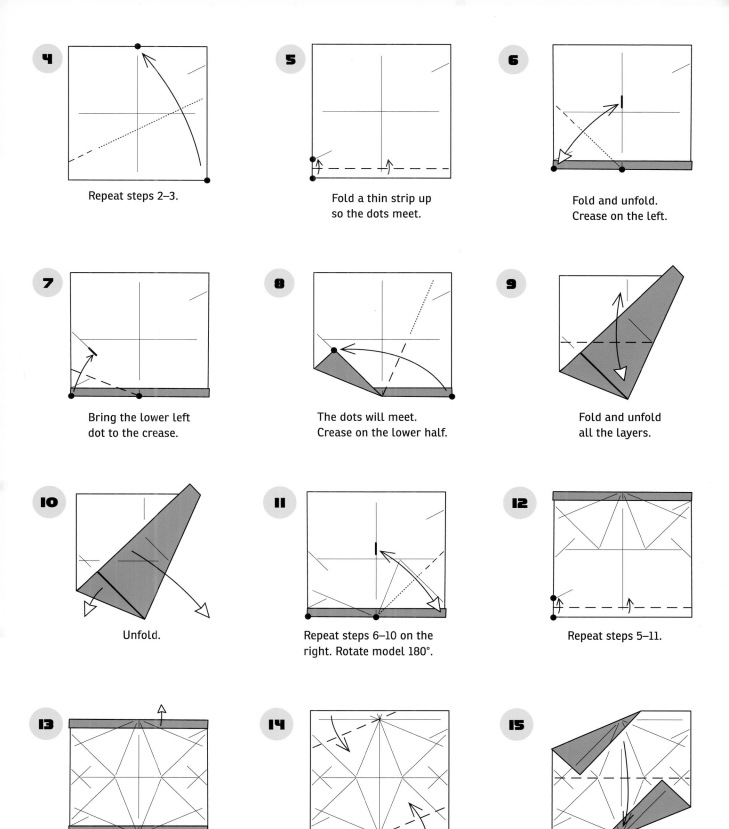

4 Repeat steps 2–3.

5 Fold a thin strip up so the dots meet.

6 Fold and unfold. Crease on the left.

7 Bring the lower left dot to the crease.

8 The dots will meet. Crease on the lower half.

9 Fold and unfold all the layers.

10 Unfold.

11 Repeat steps 6–10 on the right. Rotate model 180°.

12 Repeat steps 5–11.

13 Unfold.

14 Fold along the creases.

15 Fold in half.

16

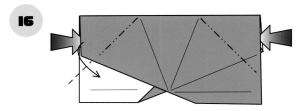

Reverse folds.

17

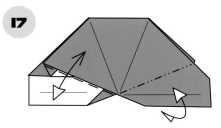

Fold and unfold.

18

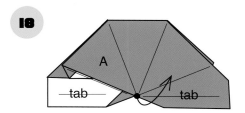

The dot will go to the right and the same below will go to the left. Follow region A.

19

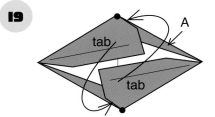

This is 3D. Tuck and interlock the tabs. The dots will meet.

20

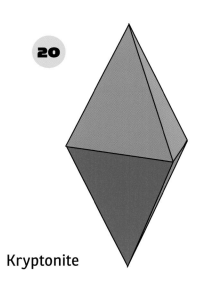

Kryptonite

SUN

Moments before his home planet exploded, young Superman escaped by rocketing to Earth aboard a small, high-tech spaceship. After his arrival, Jonathan and Martha Kent, a loving couple in Kansas, adopted the child. Soon they discovered their growing boy's extraordinary abilities of flight, freeze breath, heat vision, X-ray vision, and super-strength. Little did they know, the Earth's yellow Sun actually fueled each of these superpowers. In fact, all Kryptonians experience the same benefits from Earth's Sun, including the Man of Steel's cousin, Supergirl.

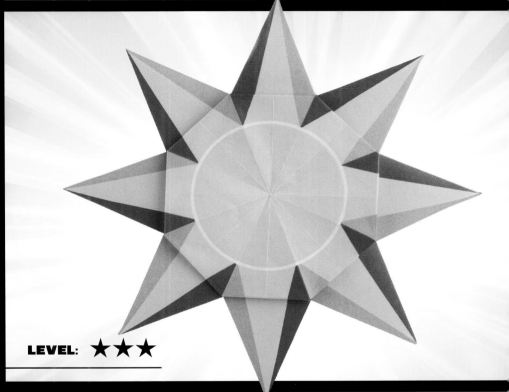

LEVEL: ★ ★ ★

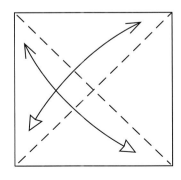

Fold and unfold.

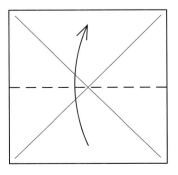

Fold in half.

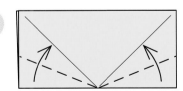

Fold to the creases.

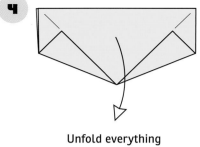

4

Unfold everything and rotate model.

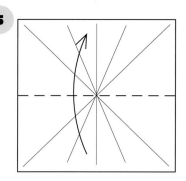

5

Repeat steps 2–4.

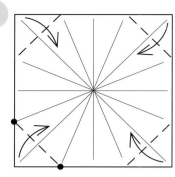

6

Fold the corners.

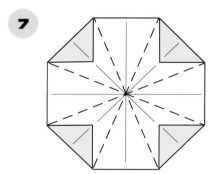

7

Fold and unfold along the creases.

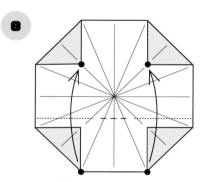

8

Fold up so the dots meet. Crease in the center.

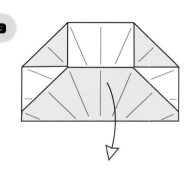

9

Unfold and rotate model.

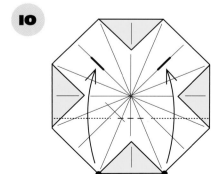

10

Fold up so the dots meet the bold lines. Crease in the center.

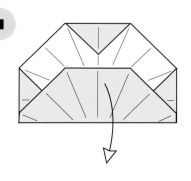

11

Unfold and rotate model.

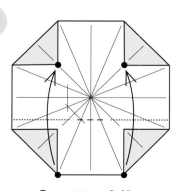

12

Repeat steps 8–11 three times.

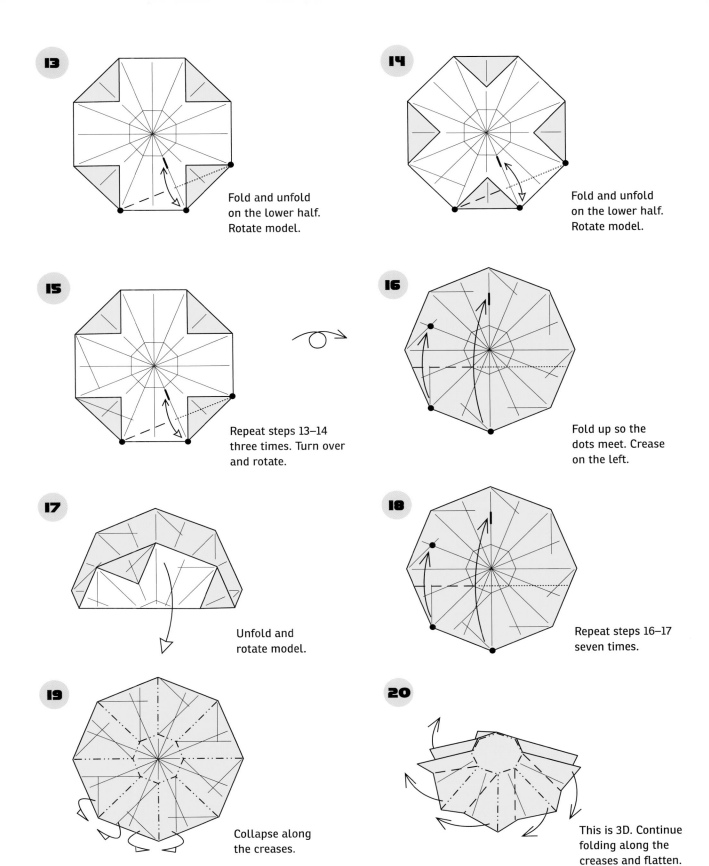

13 Fold and unfold on the lower half. Rotate model.

14 Fold and unfold on the lower half. Rotate model.

15 Repeat steps 13–14 three times. Turn over and rotate.

16 Fold up so the dots meet. Crease on the left.

17 Unfold and rotate model.

18 Repeat steps 16–17 seven times.

19 Collapse along the creases.

20 This is 3D. Continue folding along the creases and flatten.

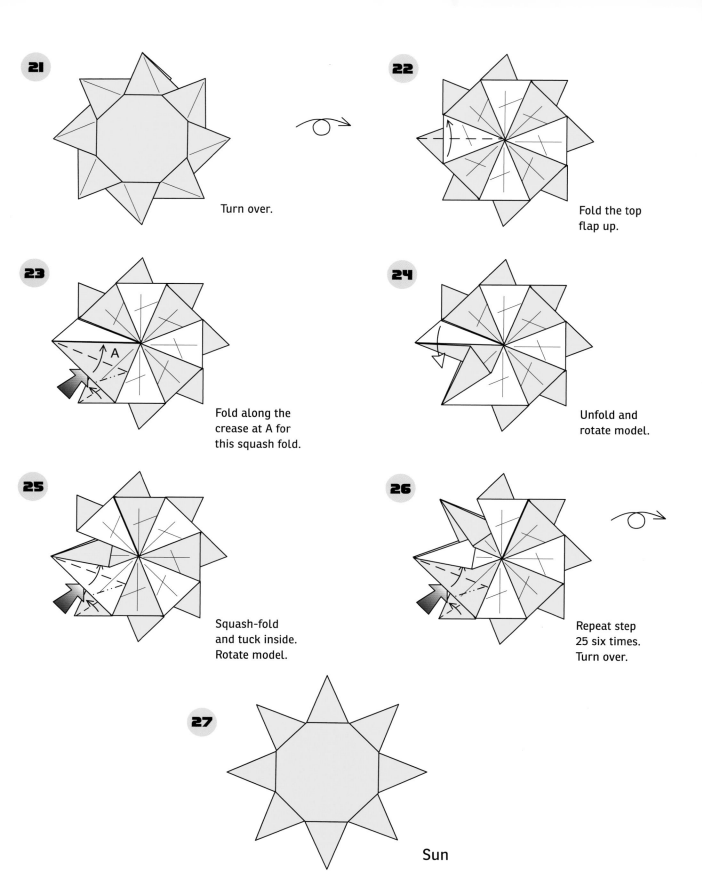

21

Turn over.

22

Fold the top
flap up.

23

A

Fold along the
crease at A for
this squash fold.

24

Unfold and
rotate model.

25

Squash-fold
and tuck inside.
Rotate model.

26

Repeat step
25 six times.
Turn over.

27

Sun

S-SHIELD

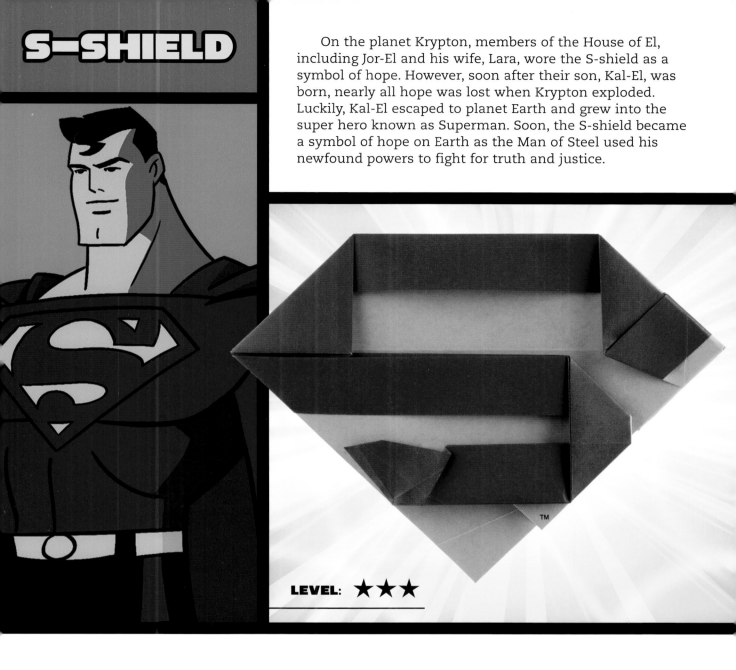

On the planet Krypton, members of the House of El, including Jor-El and his wife, Lara, wore the S-shield as a symbol of hope. However, soon after their son, Kal-El, was born, nearly all hope was lost when Krypton exploded. Luckily, Kal-El escaped to planet Earth and grew into the super hero known as Superman. Soon, the S-shield became a symbol of hope on Earth as the Man of Steel used his newfound powers to fight for truth and justice.

LEVEL: ★★★

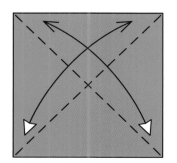

1

Fold and unfold.

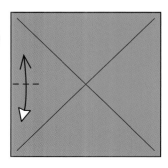

2

Fold and unfold
in half on the left.

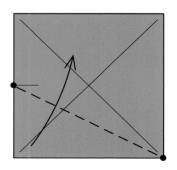

3

Fold up.

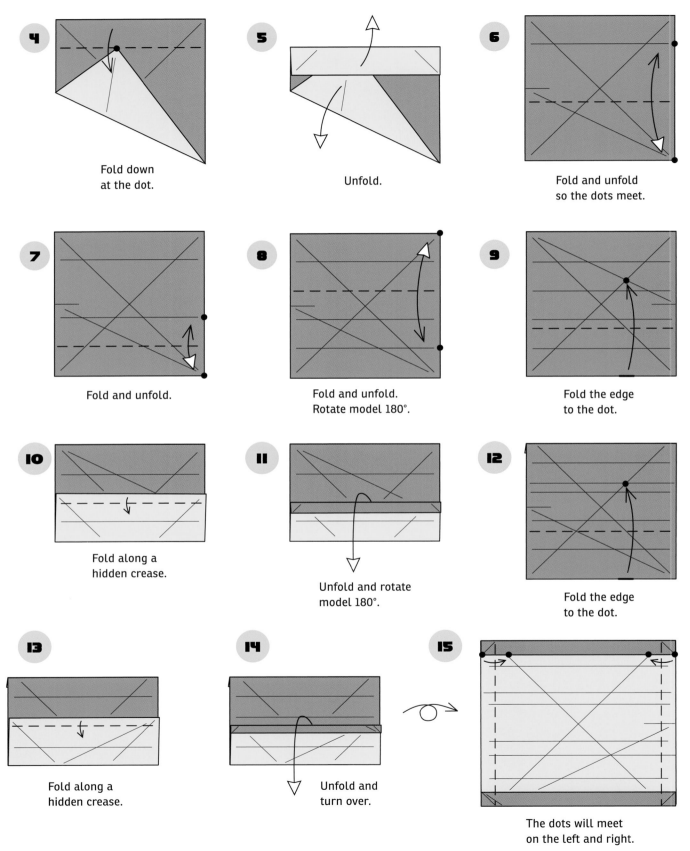

4 Fold down at the dot.

5 Unfold.

6 Fold and unfold so the dots meet.

7 Fold and unfold.

8 Fold and unfold. Rotate model 180°.

9 Fold the edge to the dot.

10 Fold along a hidden crease.

11 Unfold and rotate model 180°.

12 Fold the edge to the dot.

13 Fold along a hidden crease.

14 Unfold and turn over.

15 The dots will meet on the left and right.

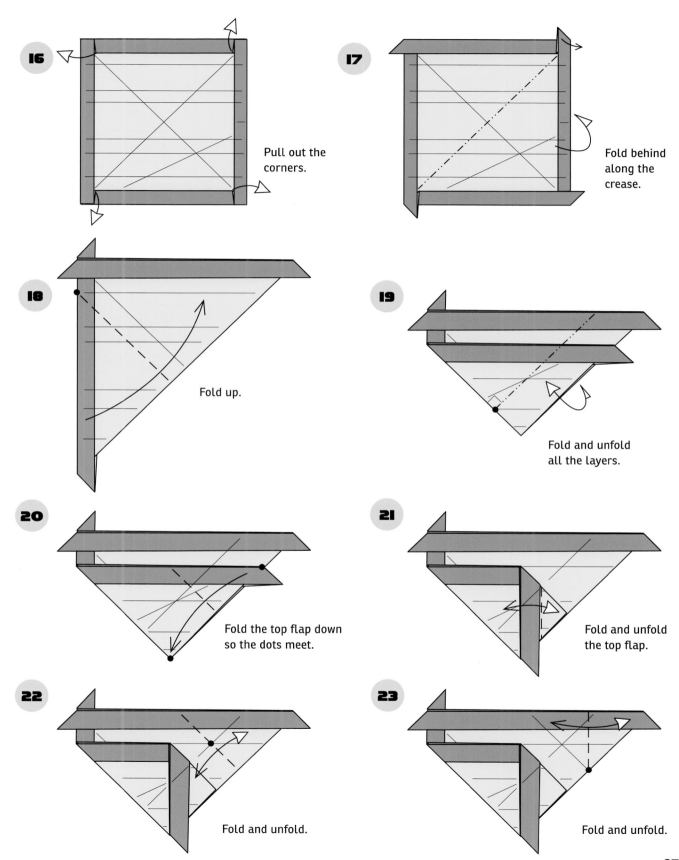

16 Pull out the corners.

17 Fold behind along the crease.

18 Fold up.

19 Fold and unfold all the layers.

20 Fold the top flap down so the dots meet.

21 Fold and unfold the top flap.

22 Fold and unfold.

23 Fold and unfold.

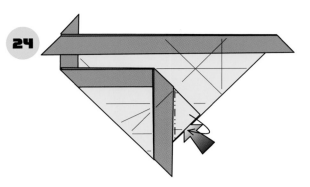

24

Reverse-fold.

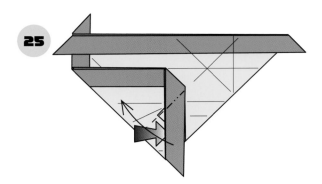

25

Reverse-fold.

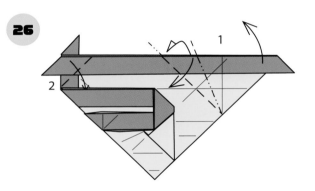

26

1. Crimp-fold.
2. Tuck between the layers.

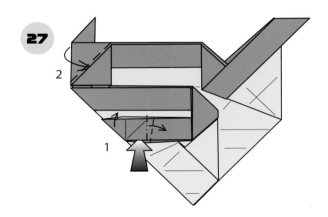

27

1. Spread-squash-fold.
2. Tuck inside.

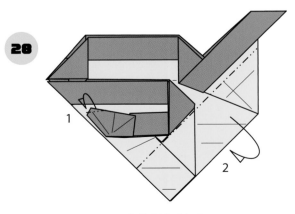

28

1. Fold behind.
2. Fold behind.
Turn over.

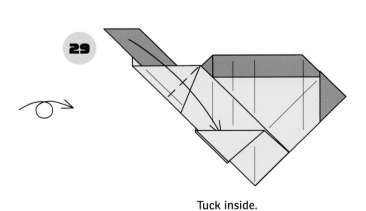

29

Tuck inside.

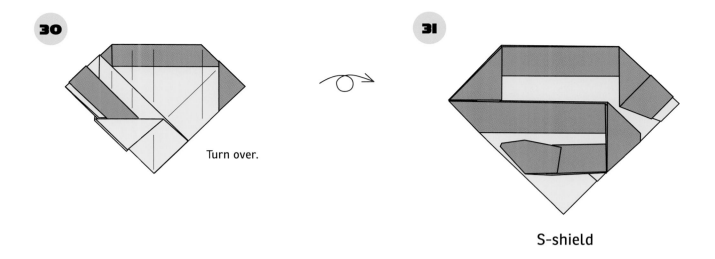

30

Turn over.

31

S-shield

To fold the Bizarro S-shield, begin with step 16 of the S-shield.

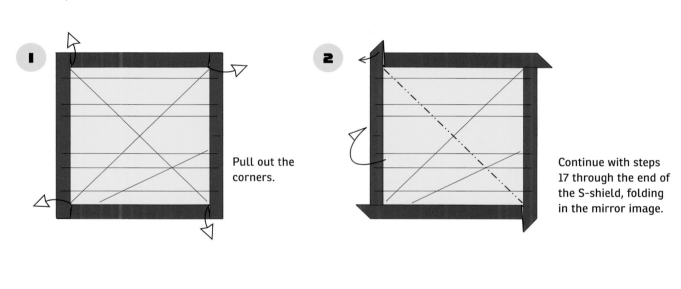

1

Pull out the corners.

2

Continue with steps 17 through the end of the S-shield, folding in the mirror image.

3

Bizarro S-shield

KRYPTO

As a young pup, Krypto grew up on the planet Krypton, Superman's home world. Just weeks before Krypton exploded, the Super-Dog escaped aboard an experimental rocket ship. On Earth, the yellow Sun gave Krypto the same superpowers as his master, the Man of Steel. With these powers, Krypto the Super-Dog leads the Space Canine Patrol Agents, a group of powerful pooches who protect the universe from evil. But, first and foremost, he's the Man of Steel's best friend.

LEVEL: ★★★

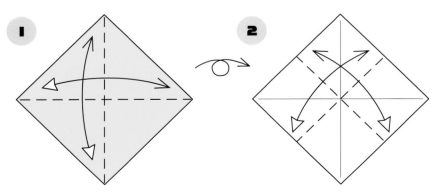

1

Fold and unfold.
Turn over.

2

Fold and unfold.

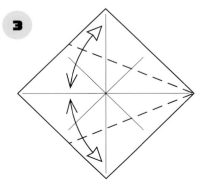

3

Fold to the center and unfold.

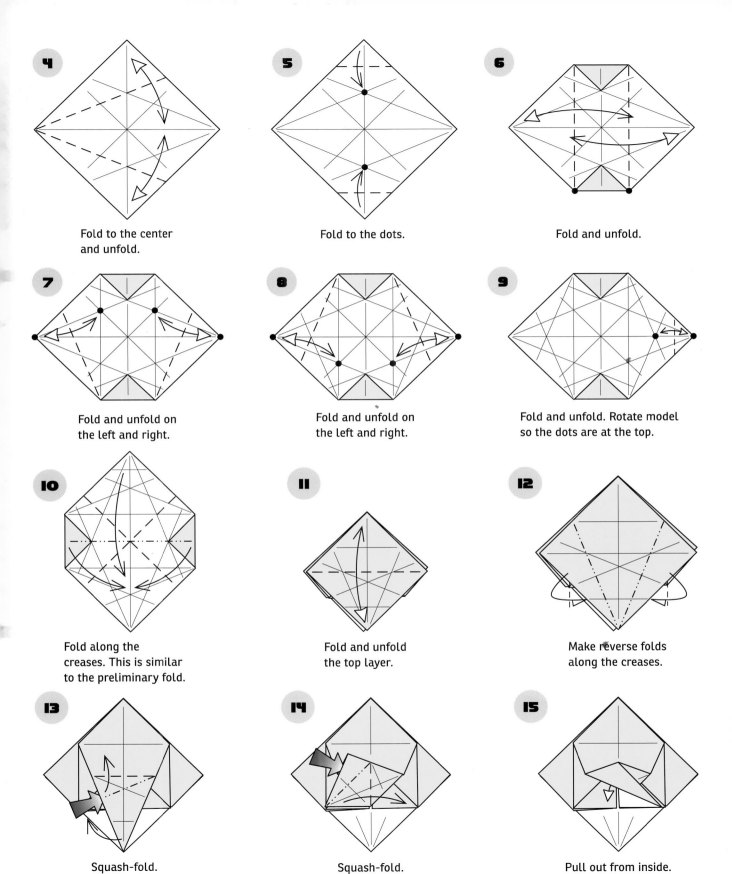

4 Fold to the center and unfold.

5 Fold to the dots.

6 Fold and unfold.

7 Fold and unfold on the left and right.

8 Fold and unfold on the left and right.

9 Fold and unfold. Rotate model so the dots are at the top.

10 Fold along the creases. This is similar to the preliminary fold.

11 Fold and unfold the top layer.

12 Make reverse folds along the creases.

13 Squash-fold.

14 Squash-fold.

15 Pull out from inside.

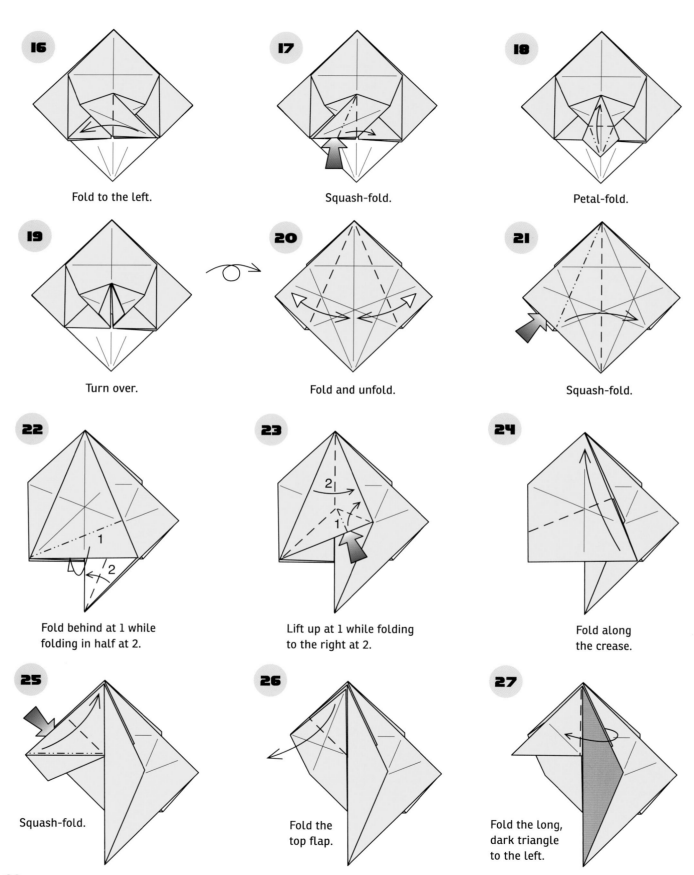

16 Fold to the left.

17 Squash-fold.

18 Petal-fold.

19 Turn over.

20 Fold and unfold.

21 Squash-fold.

22 Fold behind at 1 while folding in half at 2.

23 Lift up at 1 while folding to the right at 2.

24 Fold along the crease.

25 Squash-fold.

26 Fold the top flap.

27 Fold the long, dark triangle to the left.

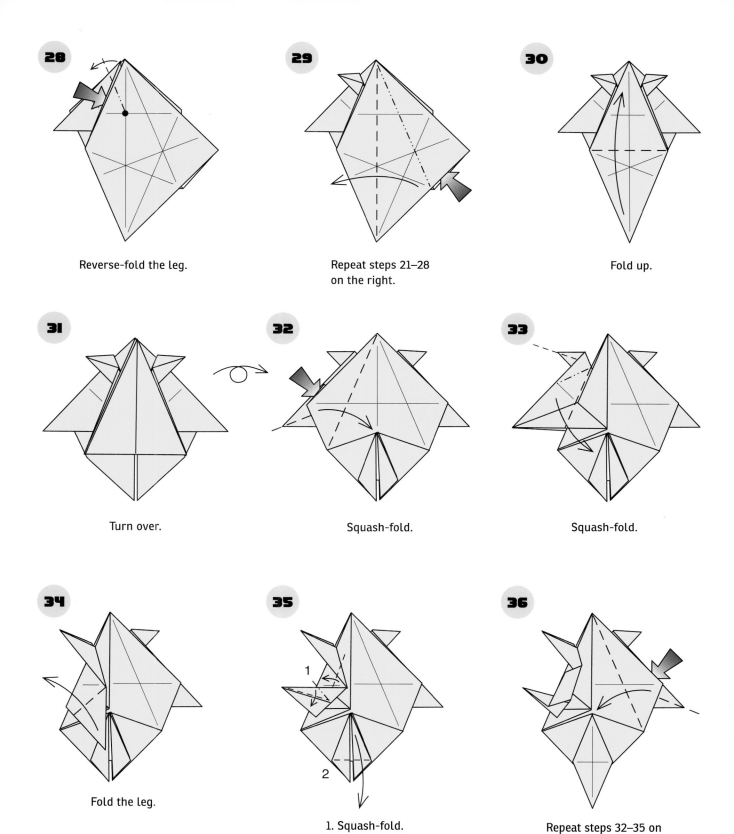

28 Reverse-fold the leg.

29 Repeat steps 21–28 on the right.

30 Fold up.

31 Turn over.

32 Squash-fold.

33 Squash-fold.

34 Fold the leg.

35
1. Squash-fold.
2. Fold down.

36 Repeat steps 32–35 on the right for the legs.

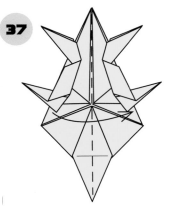

37

Fold in half and rotate model.

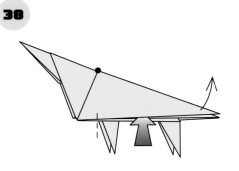

38

Pivot at the dot to slide the cape.

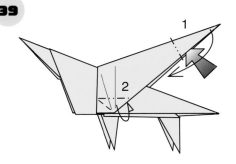

39

1. Reverse-fold.
2. Fold inside, repeat behind.

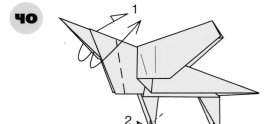

40

1. Outside-reverse-fold.
2. Reverse-fold, repeat behind.

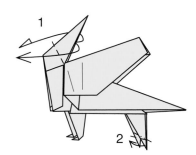

41

1. Outside-reverse-fold.
2. Crimp-fold, repeat behind.

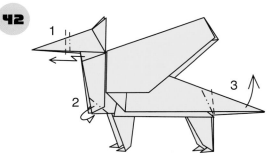

42

1. Crimp-fold.
2. Fold inside, repeat behind.
3. Crimp-fold.

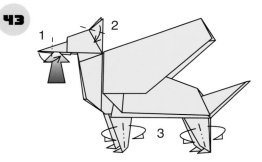

43

1. Reverse-fold.
2. Fold the ear down, repeat behind.
3. Thin and shape the legs, repeat behind.

44

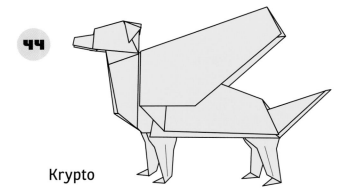

Krypto

LEX LUTHOR

Lex Luthor is one of the richest and most powerful people in all of Metropolis. To most he's simply a successful businessman. But Superman knows Luthor's dirty little secret—behind the scenes he is actually a criminal mastermind! Superman has stopped many of Luthor's sinister schemes, but Lex is careful to avoid getting caught red-handed. While Lex wants to control Superman to strengthen his grip on Metropolis, the Man of Steel is immune to Luthor's influence.

LEVEL: ★ ★ ★

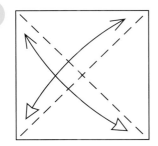

1

Fold and unfold.

2

Fold and unfold to the center. Turn over.

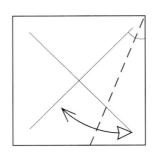

3

Fold and unfold on the diagonal.

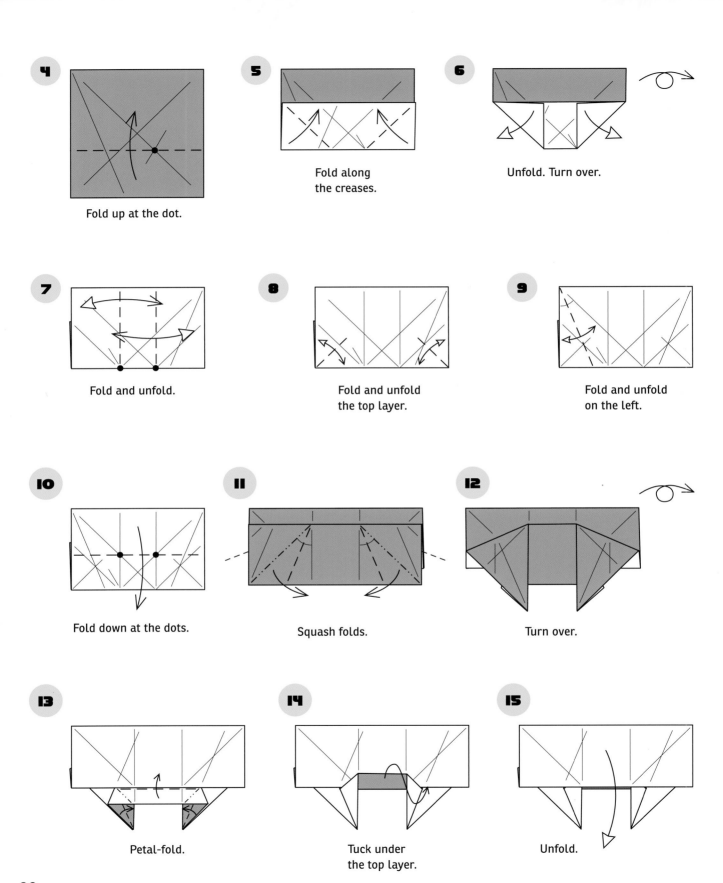

4 Fold up at the dot.

5 Fold along the creases.

6 Unfold. Turn over.

7 Fold and unfold.

8 Fold and unfold the top layer.

9 Fold and unfold on the left.

10 Fold down at the dots.

11 Squash folds.

12 Turn over.

13 Petal-fold.

14 Tuck under the top layer.

15 Unfold.

16

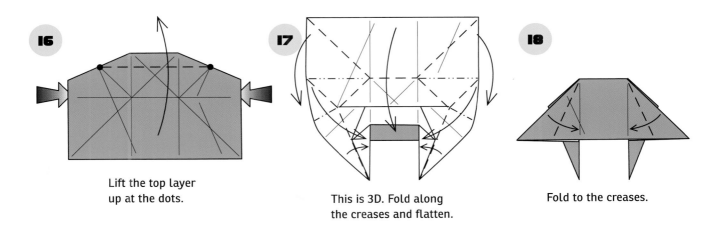

Lift the top layer
up at the dots.

17

This is 3D. Fold along
the creases and flatten.

18

Fold to the creases.

19

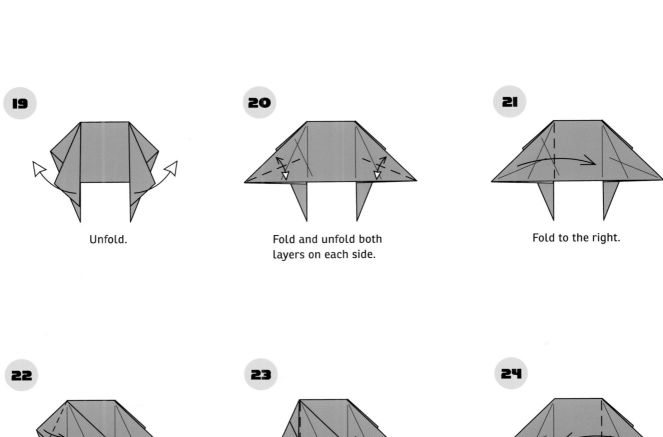

Unfold.

20

Fold and unfold both
layers on each side.

21

Fold to the right.

22

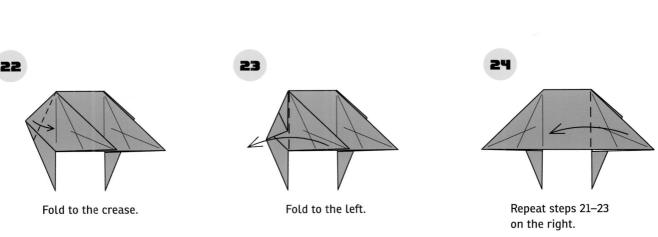

Fold to the crease.

23

Fold to the left.

24

Repeat steps 21–23
on the right.

25

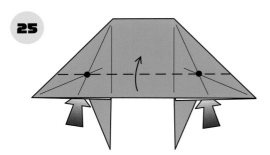

Make two squash folds
while folding up.

26

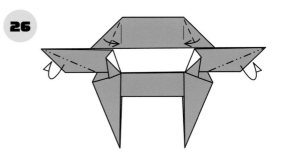

Fold along the creases.

27

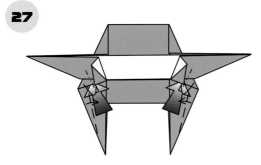

Reverse folds.

28

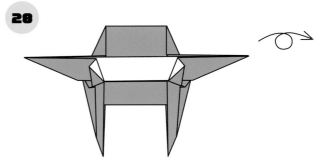

Turn over.

29

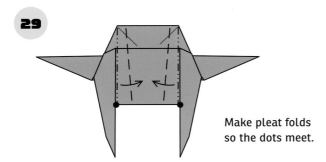

Make pleat folds
so the dots meet.

30

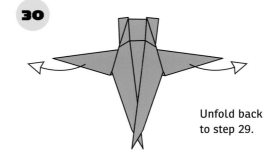

Unfold back
to step 29.

31

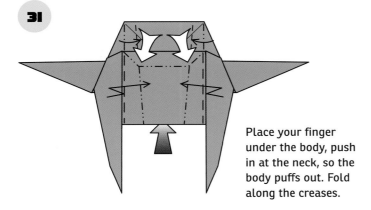

Place your finger
under the body, push
in at the neck, so the
body puffs out. Fold
along the creases.

32

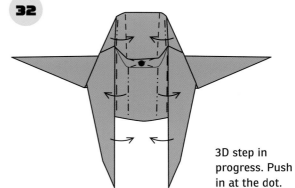

3D step in
progress. Push
in at the dot.

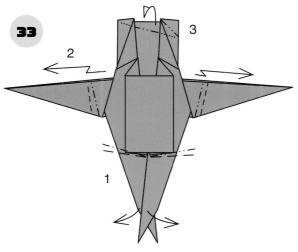

33

1. Crimp-fold the legs.
2. Crimp-fold the arms.
3. Squash-fold behind.

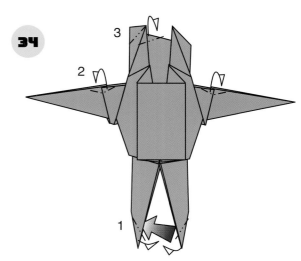

34

1. Squash-fold behind.
2. Fold inside, repeat behind.
3. Squash-fold behind.

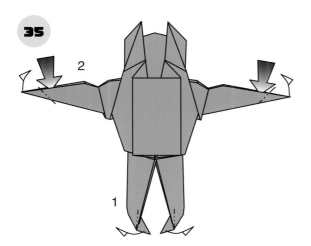

35

1. Fold the feet.
2. Squash-fold the hands from behind.

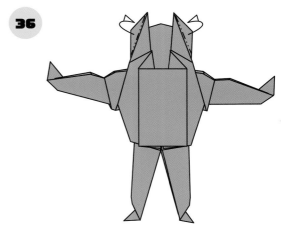

36

Fold behind.

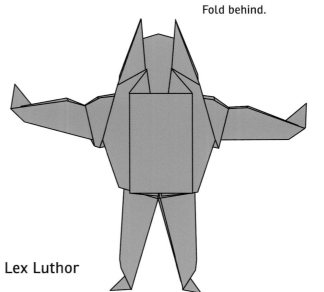

37

Lex Luthor

SUPERMAN

An infant from an exploding planet. An orphan with amazing abilities above and beyond his peers. An alien teenager who kept an out-of-this-world secret. A bespectacled newspaper reporter who always scooped the biggest stories. Epic at any age, Superman is the World's Greatest Super Hero. He survived a doomed world to make our planet his new home. His powers and courageous heart are always on call to vanquish the evil, subdue the oppressors, defend the helpless, and protect the innocent. While others may strive to follow his lead or imitate his greatness, Superman is the ultimate hero.

LEVEL: ★★★

Fold and unfold.

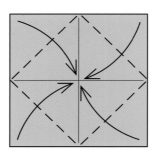

Fold to the center.

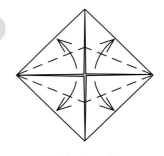

Fold to the edge.

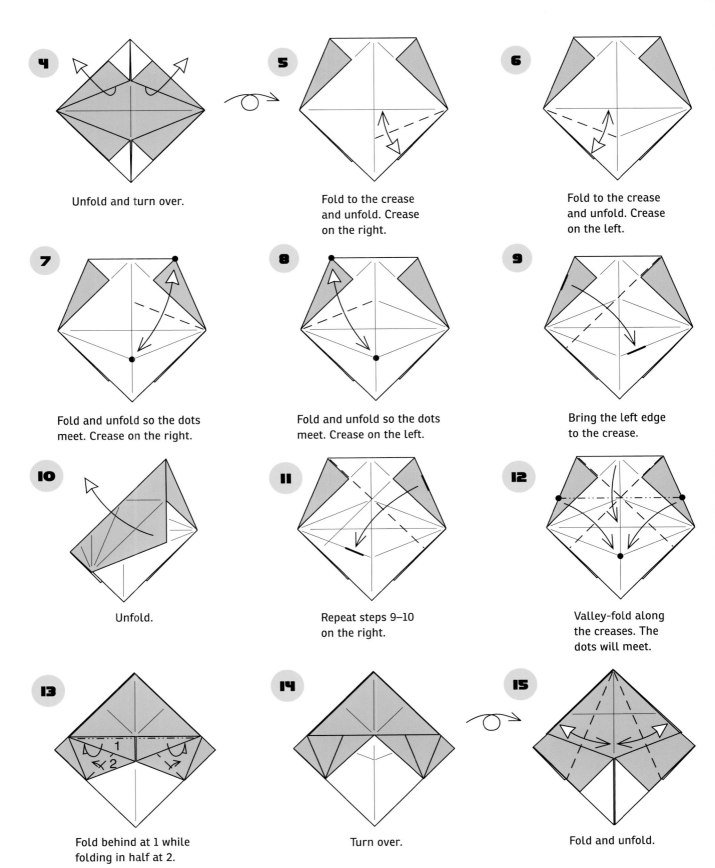

4

Unfold and turn over.

5

Fold to the crease and unfold. Crease on the right.

6

Fold to the crease and unfold. Crease on the left.

7

Fold and unfold so the dots meet. Crease on the right.

8

Fold and unfold so the dots meet. Crease on the left.

9

Bring the left edge to the crease.

10

Unfold.

11

Repeat steps 9–10 on the right.

12

Valley-fold along the creases. The dots will meet.

13

Fold behind at 1 while folding in half at 2.

14

Turn over.

15

Fold and unfold.

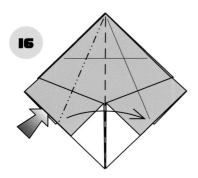

16

Squash-fold.

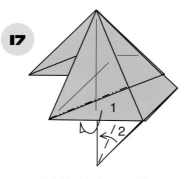

17

Fold behind at 1 while folding in half at 2.

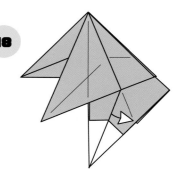

18

Pull out the hidden flap.

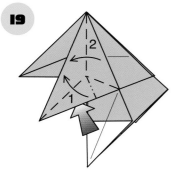

19

Lift up at 1 while folding to the left at 2.

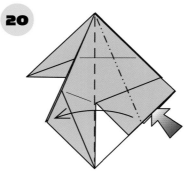

20

Repeat steps 16–19 on the right.

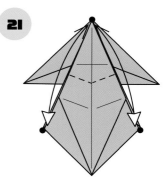

21

Fold and unfold on the left and right so the dots meet at the top.

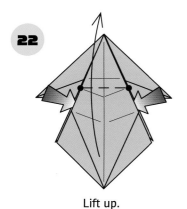

22

Lift up.

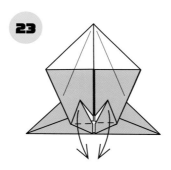

23

This is 3D. Fold down and flatten.

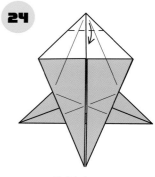

24

Fold down.

25

Fold and unfold.

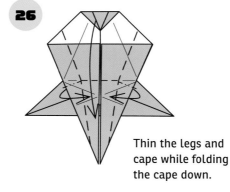

26

Thin the legs and cape while folding the cape down.

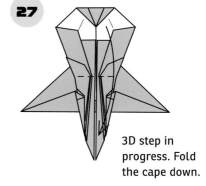

27

3D step in progress. Fold the cape down.

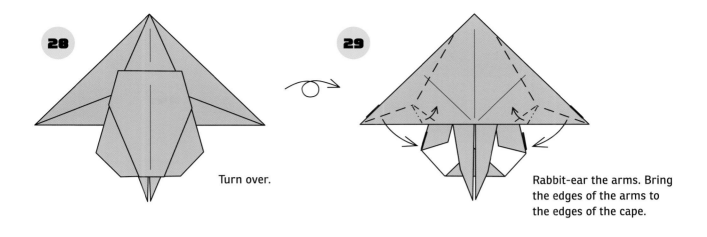

28 Turn over.

29 Rabbit-ear the arms. Bring the edges of the arms to the edges of the cape.

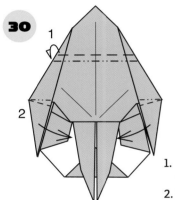

30
1. Pleat-fold between the body and cape.
2. Crimp-fold the arms.

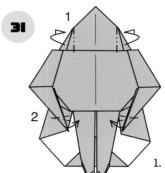

31
1. Fold behind and make small hidden squash folds at the neck.
2. Squash folds.
3. Reverse-fold and spread the feet.

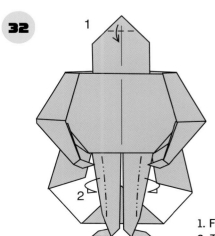

32
1. Fold down.
2. Thin and shape the legs.

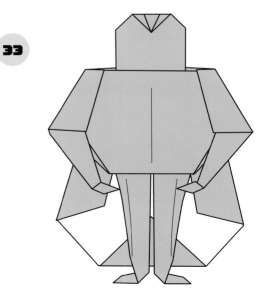

33

Superman

SUPERMAN FLYING

Look! Up in the sky! It's a bird! It's a plane! It's Superman! The Man of Steel came to Earth as an infant, rocketing to safety before his planet, Krypton, exploded. His father, the scientist Jor-El, knew that Earth's lower gravity and yellow Sun would grant his son, Kal-El, abilities far beyond those of mortal humans. The most striking ability is the power to fly. Superman can circle the globe in seconds. His uniform, made of Kryptonian materials from that early rocket ship, resists the friction of Earth's atmosphere and never burns up. The hero's familiar red and blue blur is a welcome sight as he arcs across the sky on a never-ending fight for truth and justice.

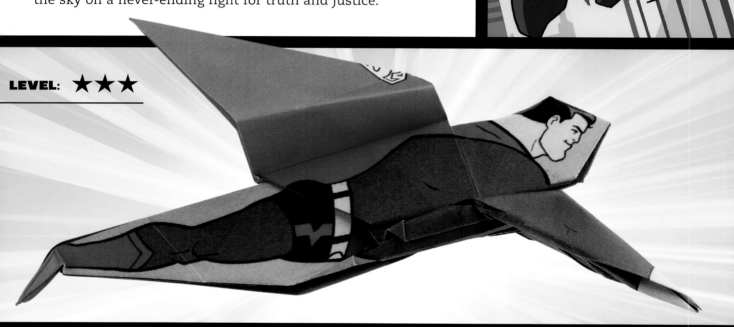

LEVEL: ★★★

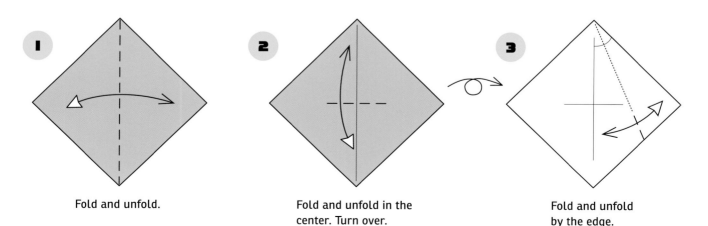

1

Fold and unfold.

2

Fold and unfold in the center. Turn over.

3

Fold and unfold by the edge.

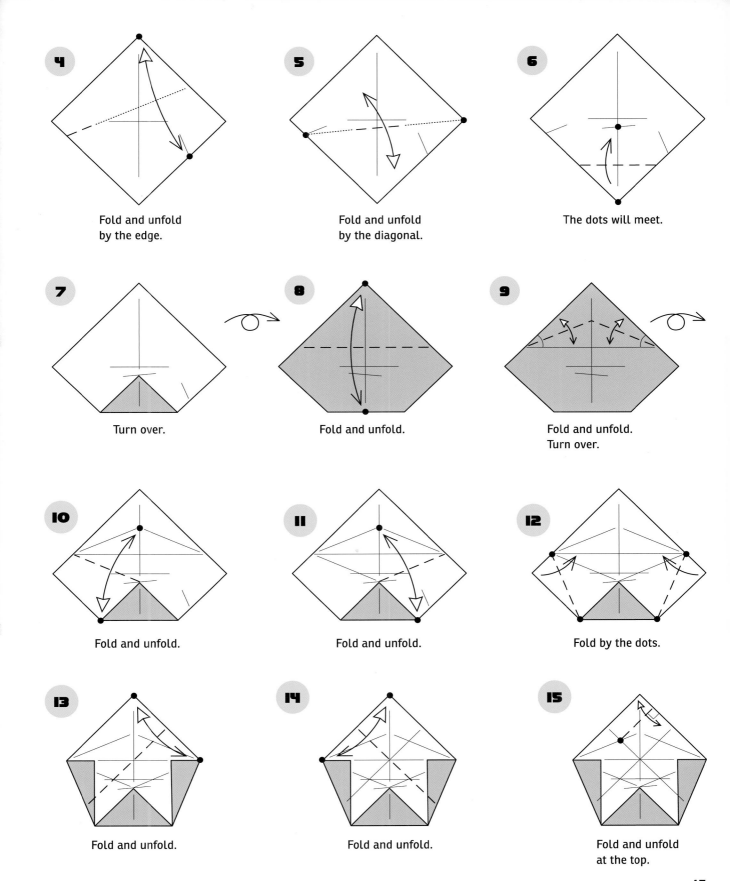

4 Fold and unfold by the edge.

5 Fold and unfold by the diagonal.

6 The dots will meet.

7 Turn over.

8 Fold and unfold.

9 Fold and unfold. Turn over.

10 Fold and unfold.

11 Fold and unfold.

12 Fold by the dots.

13 Fold and unfold.

14 Fold and unfold.

15 Fold and unfold at the top.

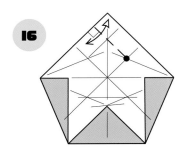

16

Fold and unfold
at the top.

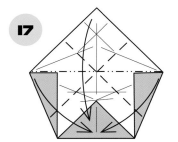

17

This is similar to the
preliminary fold.

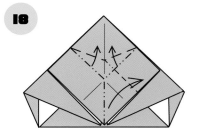

18

Fold along the
creases and flatten.

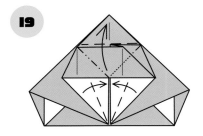

19

Petal-fold.

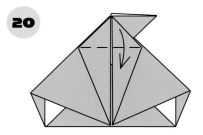

20

Fold down.

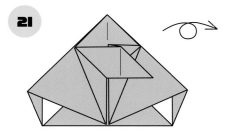

21

Turn over.

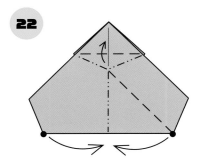

22

Fold along the creases.
The dots will meet.

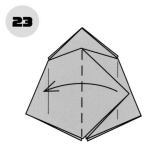

23

Fold to the left.

24

Reverse-fold.

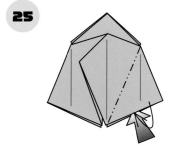

25

Reverse-fold.

26

Reverse-fold
hidden layers.

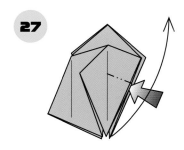

27

Reverse-fold.

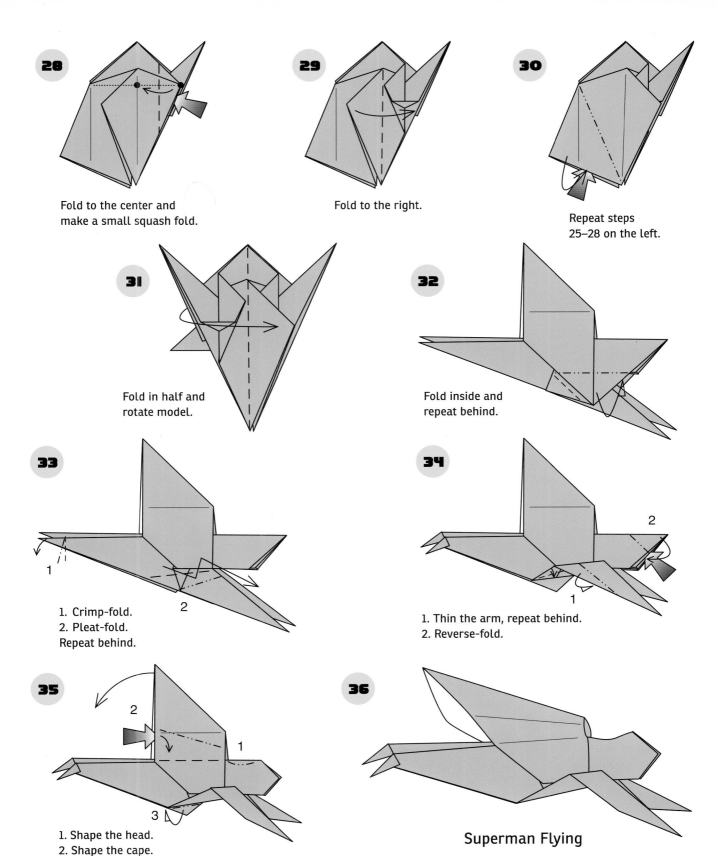

28 Fold to the center and make a small squash fold.

29 Fold to the right.

30 Repeat steps 25–28 on the left.

31 Fold in half and rotate model.

32 Fold inside and repeat behind.

33
1. Crimp-fold.
2. Pleat-fold.
Repeat behind.

34
1. Thin the arm, repeat behind.
2. Reverse-fold.

35
1. Shape the head.
2. Shape the cape.
3. Fold inside.

36 Superman Flying

Read More

Harbo, Christopher. *Origami Explosion: Scorpions, Whales, Boxes, and More!* Origami Paperpalooza. North Mankato, Minn.: Capstone Press, 2015.

Jackson, Paul. *Origami Toys: That Tumble, Fly, and Spin.* Layton, Utah: Gibbs Smith, 2010.

Montroll, John. *Origami Birds.* Mineola, N.Y.: Dover Publications, 2013.

Montroll, John. *Wonder Woman Origami: Amazing Folding Projects Featuring the Warrior Princess.* DC Origami. North Mankato, Minn.: Capstone Press, 2015.

Internet Sites

FactHound offers a safe, fun way to find Internet sites related to this book. All of the sites on FactHound have been researched by our staff.

Here's all you do:

Visit *www.facthound.com*

Type in this code: 9781491417874

Super-cool stuff! Check out projects, games and lots more at www.capstonekids.com

ABOUT THE AUTHOR

John Montroll is respected for his work in origami throughout the world. His published work has significantly increased the global repertoire of original designs in origami. John is also acknowledged for developing new techniques and groundbreaking bases. The American origami master is known for being the inspiration behind the single-square, no cuts, no glue approach in origami.

John started folding in elementary school. He quickly progressed from folding models from books to creating his own designs. John has written many books, and each model that he designs has a meticulously developed folding sequence. John's long-standing experience allows him to accomplish a model in fewer steps rather than more. It is his constant endeavor to give the reader a pleasing folding experience.